Also by Eric Hobsbawm

ON EMPIRE

ON EMPIRE

America, War, and Global Supremacy

ERIC HOBSBAWM

Pantheon Books • New York

Chapter II originally appeared in *The London Review
of Books,* February 2, 2002.

Library of Congress Cataloging-in-Publication Data
Hobsbawm, E. J. (Eric J.), [date]
On empire : America, war, and global supremacy / Eric Hobsbawm.
p. cm.
Includes bibliographical references.
ISBN 978-0-375-42537-0
1. Hegemony—United States. 2. World politics—21st century.
3. Imperialism. 4. War on Terrorism, 2001– I. Title.
JZ1312.H63 2008
327.73—dc22   2007028015

www.pantheonbooks.com
Printed in the United States of America
First Edition
2 4 6 8 9 7 5 3 1

CONTENTS

The twentieth century was the most extraordinary era in the history of humanity, combining as it did unparalleled human catastrophes, substantial material improvement, and an unprecedented increase in our capacity to transform, and perhaps to destroy, the face of our planet—and even to penetrate outside it. How are we to look back at that "age of extremes" or forward at the prospects for the new era which has emerged from the old? The present collection of essays is a historian's attempt to survey, analyze, and understand the situation of the world at the start of the third millennium and some of the main political problems confronting us today. They supplement and bring up to date what I have written in earlier publications, notably my history of the "short twentieth century" (*The Age of Extremes*), and a conversation on *On the Edge of the New Century* with Antonio

Polito. Such attempts are necessary. What can historians contribute to this task? Their main function,
apart from remembering what others have forgotten
or wish to forget, is to stand back, so far as possible,
from the contemporary record and to see it in a
broader context and in a longer perspective.

In this collection I have chosen to focus on two sets
of questions that require clear and informed thinking
today: the general question of war and peace in the
twenty-first century, and the past and future of world
empires. They take place on a world scene dominated
by two linked developments: the enormous and continuing acceleration of the ability of the human
species to change the planet by technology and economic activity, and globalization. The first of these,
unfortunately, has so far had no significant impact on
those who make political decisions. Maximizing economic growth remains the aim of governments, and
there is no realistic prospect of any effective steps
to meet the crisis of global warming. On the other
hand, since the 1960s, the accelerating advance of
globalization—that is to say, turning the world into a
single unit of interconnected activities unhampered
by local boundaries—has had a profound political
and cultural impact, especially in its currently domi-

nant form of an uncontrolled global free market. It is not specifically discussed in these essays, chiefly because politics is the one field of human activity that remains practically unaffected by it. Attempting the dubious task of quantifying it, the Swiss KOF Index of Globalization (2007) has no difficulty in finding indices of economic and information flows, personal contacts, or cultural diffusion (for instance, the number of McDonald's restaurants and IKEAs per capita), but it can think of no better measures for "political globalization" than the number of embassies in a country, its membership in international organizations, and its participation in U.N. Security Council missions. A general discussion of globalization is outside the range of this book. However, four general observations about it are particularly relevant to the book's themes.

First, the currently fashionable free-market globalization has brought about a dramatic growth in economic and social inequalities both within states and internationally. There is no sign that this polarization is not continuing within countries, in spite of a general diminution of extreme poverty. This surge of inequality, especially in the conditions of extreme economic instability such as those created by the global free market in the 1990s, is at the roots of the major social and political tensions of the new century. Insofar as international inequalities may be under pressure from the rise of the new Asian economies, both the threat to the relatively astronomic standards of living of the peoples of the old North, and the practical impossibility of achieving anything like them for the vast populations of such countries as India and China, will produce their own domestic and international tensions.

Second, the impact of this globalization is felt most by those who benefit from it least. Hence the growing polarization of views about it, between those who are potentially sheltered from its negative effects—the entrepreneurs who can outsource their costs to countries of cheap labor, the high-tech professionals, and graduates of higher education who can get work in any high-income market economy—and those who are not. That is why for most of those who live by the wages or salaries of their employment in the old "developed countries," the early twenty-first century offers a troubling, not to say sinister, prospect. The global free market has undermined the ability of their states and welfare systems to protect their way of life. In a global economy they compete with men and women abroad, of equal qualifications but paid a fraction of the Western pay packet, and at home living standards are under pressure from the globalization of what Marx called "the reserve army of labor"—immigrants from the villages of the great global zones of poverty. Situations such as this do not promise an era of political and social stability.

Third, while the actual scale of globalization remains modest, except perhaps in a number of generally smallish states, mainly in Europe, its political and cultural impact is disproportionately large. Thus, immigration is a major political problem in most developed economies of the West, even though the world share of people living in a country other than the one in which they were born is no more than 3 percent. In the KOF Index of Economic Globalization, the United States is in 39th place, Germany in 40th, China in 55th, Brazil in 60th, South Korea in 62nd, Japan in 67th, and India in 105th, though all except Brazil are somewhat higher in the ranking of "social globalization." (The United Kingdom is the only major economy in the top ten of both economic and social globalization.)[1] While it may or may not be a historically temporary phenomenon, in the short term this disproportionately large impact may well

have serious national and international political consequences. I would guess that, in one way or another,
political resistance, though unlikely to revive formal
protectionist policies, is likely to slow down the
progress of free-market globalization in the next
decade or two.

The pieces collected here, mostly given as lectures
before various audiences, try to set out and explain
the situation in which the world, or large parts of it,
finds itself today. They may help to define the problems that we confront at the start of the new century,
but they do not propose programs or practical solutions. They were written between 2000 and 2006, and
therefore reflect the specific international concerns
of that period, which was dominated by the decision
of the U.S. government in 2001 to assert a single-
handed world hegemony, denouncing hitherto
accepted international conventions, reserving its
right to launch wars of aggression or other military
operations whenever it wanted to, and actually doing
so. Given the débâcle of the Iraq War, it is no longer
necessary to demonstrate that this project was unre-
alistic, and the question whether we would have

wanted it to succeed or not is therefore entirely academic. Nevertheless, it should be evident, and readers should bear in mind, that my essays were written by an author who is deeply critical of the project. This is partly because of the strength and indestructibility of my political convictions, including a hostility to imperialism, whether of Great Powers that claim they are doing their victims a favor by conquering them or of white men assuming automatic superiority for themselves and their arrangements to those of other skin colors. It is also due to a rationally justifiable suspicion of the megalomania that is the occupational disease of states and rulers who believe there are no limits on their power or success.

Most of the arguments and lies justifying U.S. actions since 2001 by U.S. and British politicians, paid or unpaid advocates, rhetoricians, publicists, and amateur ideologists no longer need detain us. However, a less disreputable case has been made, if not for the Iraq War then for the general proposition that armed cross-border intervention to preserve or establish human rights is legitimate and sometimes necessary in an era of growing global barbarity, violence, and disorder. For some this implies the desirability of a world imperial hegemony, and specifically one exercised by the only power capable of establishing it, the United States of America. This proposition, which may be called the imperialism of human rights, entered public debate in the course of the Balkan conflicts arising out of the disintegration of communist Yugoslavia, especially in Bosnia, which seemed to suggest that only outside armed force could put an end to endless mutual massacre and that only the United States was able and willing to use such force. That the United States had no particular interests, historic, political, or economic, in the region made its intervention more impressive and apparently selfless. I have taken note of it in my essays. Though my essays contain reasons for rejecting it, some additional observations on this position may not be out of place.

Justification for such intervention is fundamentally flawed by the fact that Great Powers in the pursuit of their international policies may do things that suit the champions of human rights, and be aware of the publicity value of doing so, but that this is quite incidental to their purposes, which, if they think it necessary, are today pursued with the ruthless barbarism that is the heritage of the twentieth century. Those for whom a great human cause is central can be in a relationship of alliance or opposition with a state, but never of permanent identification. Even the rare case of young revolutionary states genuinely seeking to spread their universal message—France after 1792, Russia after 1917, but not, as it happens, George Washington's isolationist America—is always short-lived. The default position of any state is to pursue its interests.

Beyond this, the humanitarian case for armed intervention in the affairs of states rests on three assumptions: that intolerable situations may arise in the contemporary world—usually massacre or even genocide—which call for it; that no other ways of dealing with them is possible; and that the benefits of intervening are patently greater than the costs. All these assumptions are sometimes justified, although, as the debate on Iraq and Iran proves, there is rarely universal agreement about what precisely constitutes an "intolerable situation." Probably there was consensus in the two most obvious cases of justified intervention: the invasion of Cambodia by Vietnam that put an end to the appalling regime of Pol Pot's "killing fields" (1978) and the destruction of Idi Amin's regime of terror in Uganda by Tanzania (1979). (Not all rapid and successful foreign armed interventions in local crisis situations have produced such satisfactory results—for example, Liberia and East Timor.) Both were achieved by brief incursions, produced immediate benefits and probably some lasting improvements, while implying no systematic abrogation of the established principle of noninterference in the internal affairs of sovereign states. Incidentally, they had no imperial implications, nor did they involve wider world politics. Indeed, both the United States and China continued to support the deposed Pol Pot. Such ad hoc interventions are irrelevant to the case for the desirability of a world hegemony by the United States.

The same cannot be said of the armed interventions of recent years, which have been selective, not touching what by humanitarian standards were some of the very worst examples of atrocity, notably the Central African genocide. In the Balkans of the 1990s, humanitarian concern was certainly a significant factor, though not the only one. Probably, though the opposite has been argued, outside intervention helped to end the local bloodshed in Bosnia earlier than if the war between Serbs, Croats, and Bosnian Moslems had been allowed to continue to its conclusion, but the region remains unsettled. It is by no means clear whether in 1999 armed intervention was the only way to settle the problems raised by a rebellion against Serbia of an extremist minority group among Albanian nationalists in Kosovo. The humanitarian basis for the action was rather more doubtful than in Bosnia and, by provoking Serbia into the mass expulsion of the Kosovo Albanians, as well as by the civilian casualties of the war itself and some months of destructive bombing of Serbia, it may actually have made the humanitarian situation worse. Nor have relations between Serbs and Albanians been stabilized. At least the Balkan interventions were rapid, and in the short run decisive, though so far nobody, except perhaps Croatia, has reason to feel satisfied with the outcome.

On the other hand, the wars in Afghanistan and Iraq since 2001 were U.S. military operations not undertaken for humanitarian reasons, though justified to humanitarian public opinion on the ground that they removed some rather unsavory regimes. But for 9/11, not even America would have regarded the situation in either country as calling for immediate invasion. Afghanistan was accepted by other states on old-fashioned "realist" grounds; Iraq was almost universally condemned. Though the Taliban and Saddam Hussein's regimes were rapidly over-thrown, neither war achieved victory, and certainly neither achieved the aims announced at the out-set, the establishment of democratic regimes in line with Western values, a beacon to other as-yet-undemocratized societies in the region. Both, but especially the catastrophic Iraq War, proved to be lengthy, massively destructive, and bloody, and both still continue at the time this is written without a prospect of conclusion.

In all these cases, armed intervention has come from foreign states with far superior military power and resources. In none of them has it so far produced stable solutions. In all the countries concerned, for-eign military occupation and political supervision continue. In the best of cases—but plainly not in Afghanistan and Iraq—intervention has ended bloody wars and produced some kind of peace, but the positive results, as in the Balkans, are disappoint-ing. In the worst of cases—Iraq—nobody would seri-ously deny that for the people whose liberation was the official excuse for the war, the situation is worse than before. The recent record of armed interven-tions in the affairs of other countries, even by super-powers, is not one of success.

Its failure is based partly on an assumption which also lies behind much of the imperialism of human rights: that regimes of barbarity and tyranny are immune to internal change, so that only outside force can bring about their end and the consequent diffusion of our values and political or legal institutions. This assumption is inherited from the days when Cold Warriors denounced "totalitarianism." It should not have survived the end of the U.S.S.R.—which was internally generated and not externally imposed—or, for that matter, the evident process of relatively successful internal democratization after 1980 in several once unsavory noncommunist authoritarian, militarist, and dictatorial regimes in Asia and South America. It is also based on the belief that acts of force can instantly bring about major cultural transformations. But this is not so.

The diffusion of values and institutions can hardly ever be brought about by a sudden imposition by outside force, unless conditions are already present locally which make them adaptable and their introduction acceptable. Democracy and Western values and human rights are not like some technological importations whose benefits are immediately obvious and will be adopted in the same manner by all who can use them and afford them, like the peaceful bicycle and the murderous AK-47, or technical services like airports. If they were, there would be more political similarity between the numerous states of Europe, Asia, and Africa that all live under similar democratic constitutions in theory, but by no means in practice. In a word, there are very few shortcuts in history: a lesson which the author has learned, not least, from living through and reflecting on much of the past century.

Finally, a word of thanks to those who provided the occasion for the first presentation of these studies. Chapter I was an inaugural address at the presentation of an honorary degree at the Aristotle University of Thessaloniki, in Greece, in 2004; chapter II is based on a paper written for a colloquium to commemorate the centenary of the Nobel Peace Prize (Oslo, 2001); chapter III is based on the Nikhil Chakravarty Memorial Lecture given in Delhi in 2004, by invitation of the *Indian Review of Books;* and chapter IV was the William E. Massey, Sr., Lecture at Harvard University in 2005.

ON EMPIRE

I

On the End of Empires

When I was born, all Europeans lived in states which were part of empires in the traditional monarchical or the nineteenth-century colonial sense of the world, except the citizens of Switzerland, the three Scandinavian states, and the former dependencies of the Ottoman Empire in the Balkans—and some of these had left the Ottoman Empire only just before the First World War. The inhabitants of Africa lived under empires almost without exception, and so, without any exception, did the inhabitants of the Pacific and Southeast Asian islands, large and small. But for the fact that the ancient Chinese Empire had come to an end some six years before I was born, one might have said that all the countries of Asia were parts of empires, old and new, except perhaps Thailand (then known as Siam) and Afghanistan, maintaining a sort of independence between rival European powers. Only the Americas south of the United States consisted primarily of states which neither had nor were colonial dependencies, even though they were certainly economically and culturally dependent.

In the course of my lifetime all this has gone. The First World War broke the Habsburg Empire into fragments and completed the breakup of the Ottoman Empire. But for the October Revolution, this would also have been the fate of the empire of the Russian tsar, though it was severely weakened, as was the German Empire, which lost both the imperial title and its colonies. The Second World War destroyed the imperial potential of Germany, which had been briefly realized under Adolf Hitler. It destroyed the colonial empires of the imperialist era, great and small, the British, French, and Japanese, the Dutch and Portuguese, the Belgian, and what little remained of the Spanish. Incidentally, it also brought the end of the relatively brief U.S. excursion into formal colonialism on the European model, in the Philippines and a few other territories. Finally, at the end of the last century, the collapse of European communist regimes brought to an end both Russia as a single multinational entity as it had existed under the tsars and the more short-lived Soviet Empire in East and Central Europe. The metropoles have lost their power, as they have lost their dependencies. Only one potential imperial power remains.

Thirty years ago, most of us welcomed this dramatic change in the political face of the globe, as many of us still do. However, today we look back on it from a troubled new century that seems to lack the relative order and predictability of the Cold War era. The era of empires has gone, but so far nothing has effectively replaced it. The number of independent states has quadrupled since 1913, most of them the debris of former empires, but while in theory we now live in the world of free nation-states which, according to Presidents Wilson and Roosevelt, was to replace the world of empires, in practice we live in what we can now recognize as a deeply unstable form of global disorder both internationally and within states. A number—probably a growing number—of these political entities appear incapable of carrying on the essential functions of territorial states or are threatened with disintegration by secessionist movements. What is more, since the end of the Cold War we live in an era when uncontrollable or barely controllable armed conflict has become endemic in large areas of Asia, Africa, Europe, and parts of the Pacific. Massacre amounting to genocide and the mass expulsion of populations ("ethnic cleansing") are once again taking place on a scale not seen since the years immediately following World War II. Can we wonder that in some countries the survivors of former empires regret their passing?

How should these empires be remembered? The nature of official and popular memory depends to some extent on the length of time that has elapsed since an empire's disappearance and whether it has left any inheritors. The Roman Empire, both in its western and eastern form, was so completely destroyed, and destroyed so long ago, that it has no inheritor, though the mark it has left on the world, even outside the area it once occupied, is enormous. Alexander's is gone forever, and so is Genghis Khan's and Timur's. So are the empires of the Umayyads and Abbasids. More recently, the Habsburg Empire was so completely destroyed in 1918, and was so completely a-national in structure, that it has no effective continuity with the small nation-state now called

Austria. However, often there is some continuity, especially as the end of so many empires is so recent, and has usually been accompanied or followed, in the former metropolitan states, by periods of considerable political and psychological stress. True, today no state that once ruled over a colonial empire intends to, or has any hope of, restoration. But where the metropoles of former empires survive as effective states, usually as nation-states, there is a tendency among them after a while to look back on the times of past greatness with pride and nostalgia. There is also an understandable temptation to exaggerate the benefits which the empire is said to have conferred on its subjects while it existed, such as the law and order within its territories and, with more justification, the fact that several (but not all) vanished empires have been more tolerant of ethnic, linguistic, and religious multiplicity than the nation-states that succeeded them. Nevertheless, as a writer on empires points out, reviewing Professor Mazower's remarkable social history *Salonica, City of Ghosts: Christians, Muslims and Jews, 1430–1950,* "this theory of empire is too good to be true...."[1] The reality of empires should not be in the hands of selective nostalgia.

Only one collective form of imperial memory has

practical implications today. This is the feeling that the superior power of empires to conquer and rule the world was based on superior civilization, easily identified with moral or even racial superiority. In the nineteenth century both tended to go together, but the historical experience of Nazi Germany has eliminated racial or ethnic claims to superiority from polite discourse. However, the tacit rather than openly articulated Western claim of moral superiority remains, and finds expression in the conviction that our values and institutions are superior to others' and may, or even should, be imposed on them to their benefit, if necessary by force of arms.

The claim that historically empires and imperialism brought civilization to backward people and substituted order for anarchy is doubtful, though not entirely spurious. From the third to the seventeenth century of our era, most empires were the products of military conquest by warrior tribes from the outer edges of the Asian and Mediterranean civilizations. Culturally backward, they brought little to the conquered and often more advanced lands but their swords and, if they wanted to last, a willingness to use the infrastructure and the expertise of those they had defeated. Only the Arabs, who carried their written language and their new religion with them, brought something new. The Europeans who colonized the Americas, Africa, and the Pacific were indeed technologically superior to the local societies, though until the nineteenth century not to Asian and some Islamic ones. Colonial territories were indeed eventually integrated into an occidentalo-centric world economy. But we may well ask how positive is the balance sheet of the colonial era for the inhabitants of the Americas other than the descendants of the European immigrants who settled there. Or, to take a more recent case, for the inhabitants of sub-Saharan Africa.

The memory of empire among its former subjects is more ambiguous. Most colonies or other dependencies of former empires have been transformed into independent states, which, like all states however new and unprecedented, need a history as well as a flag. So their memory of the former empire is almost always dominated by the history of the creation of the new state, which tends to take the form of a foundation myth of struggle and liberation. Not unnaturally it also tends to take a uniformly negative view of the era of imperial rule. In most cases this calls for historical skepticism. Such narratives tend to exaggerate the independent role of the forces of liberation, to underestimate the local forces not involved in the liberation movements, and to oversimplify the relationship between an empire and its subject population. Even in countries with a long history of liberation struggle, separation from empire usually was a more complex process than official nationalist history allows. The truth is that what has brought empires to an end is rarely the revolt of their subject peoples alone.

The relation between empires and their subjects is complex, because the foundation of the power of lasting empires is also complex. Brief periods of foreign occupation may rest essentially on military power and the willingness to use coercion and terror, but these alone cannot guarantee durable foreign rule. Especially when that rule is exercised, as it almost always has been, by relatively, and indeed usually absolutely, tiny numbers of foreigners. Let us remember that the number of British civilians engaged in governing the four hundred million in the Indian Empire was never more than about ten thousand. Historically, empires may have been conquered by military force and established by terror ("shock and awe," in the phrase of the Pentagon), but if they wanted to last, they have had to rely on two main instruments—cooperation with local interests and the legitimacy of effective power—while also exploiting the disunity of their adversaries and their subjects (*divide et impera*). The present situation in Iraq illustrates the difficulties of even the most powerful occupier, when these are absent.

But for that very reason, the old era of empires cannot be revived, least of all by a single superpower. One of the major assets of Western imperialism, formal or informal, was that in the first instance "Westernization" was the only form in which backward economies could be modernized and weak states strengthened. This provided Western empires or modernizing metropoles of traditional empires with the built-in goodwill of such local elites as were interested in overcoming local backwardness. This was so even when the indigenous modernizers eventually turned against foreign rule, as in India and Egypt. Paradoxically, an official Indian national song was written by a senior native member of the Indian Civil Service of the British Raj. Yet the globalization of the industrial economy has made modernization international. South Korea has little to learn from the United States, which imports its software experts from India and exports its office work to Sri Lanka, while Brazil produces not only coffee but executive jets. Asians may still find it useful to send their children to study in the West, often to be taught there by immigrant Asian academics, but the presence of Westerners in their countries, let alone local political power and influence, are no longer needed to modernize their societies.

Yet would-be empires face an even greater handicap. They can no longer rely on the obedience of their subjects. And, thanks to the heritage of the Cold War, those who refuse to obey now have access to weapons sufficiently powerful to hold strong states at bay. In the past, countries could be ruled by a comparative handful of foreigners, because the rule of any regime with effective power was accepted by people used to being ruled from above, whether by natives or foreigners. Imperial rule, once established, was likely to be resisted only by peoples who rejected any central state power, indigenous or foreign, and who usually lived in zones like the Afghan, Berber, or Kurdish mountains, beyond effective civilian control. And even these knew that they had to coexist with the greater power of sultan, tsar, and Raj. Today, as the former French territories in Africa demonstrate, the presence of a few French troops alone is no longer enough to maintain local regimes, as it was for decades after formal decolonization. Today, the full armed power of governments has proved incapable of maintaining unchallenged control of their territory for decades—in Sri Lanka, in India's Kashmir, in Colombia, in the Gaza Strip and the West Bank, or still, for that matter, in parts of Belfast. There is, indeed, a general crisis of state power and state legitimacy even on the home territories of old and stable European states like Spain and the United Kingdom.

In these circumstances there is no prospect of a return to the imperial world of the past, let alone the prospect of a lasting global imperial hegemony, unprecedented in history, by a single state, such as America, however great its military force. The age of empires is dead. We shall have to find another way of organizing the globalized world of the twenty-first century.

II

War and Peace in the Twentieth Century

The twentieth century was the most murderous in recorded history. The total number of deaths caused by or associated with its wars has been estimated at 187 million, the equivalent of more than 10 percent of the world's population in 1913. Taken as having begun in 1914, it was a century of almost unbroken war, with few and brief periods without organized armed conflict somewhere. It was dominated by world wars: that is to say, by wars between territorial states or alliances of states. The period from 1914 to 1945 can be regarded as a single "thirty years' war" interrupted only by a pause in the 1920s—between the final withdrawal of the Japanese from the Soviet Far East in 1922 and the attack on Manchuria in 1931.

This period was followed, almost immediately, by some forty years of Cold War, which conformed to Hobbes's definition of war as consisting "not in battle only or the act of fighting, but in a tract of time wherein the will to contend by battle is sufficiently known." It is a matter for debate how far the actions in which U.S. armed forces have been involved since the end of the Cold War in various parts of the globe constitute a continuation of the era of world war. There can be no doubt, however, that the 1990s were filled with formal and informal military conflict in Europe, Africa, and Western and Central Asia. The world as a whole has not been at peace since 1914, and is not at peace now.

Nevertheless, the century cannot be treated as a single block, either chronologically or geographically. Chronologically, it falls into three periods: the era of world war centered on Germany (1914 to 1945), the era of confrontation between the two superpowers (1945 to 1989), and the era since the end of the classic international power system. I shall call these periods I, II, and III. Geographically, the impact of military operations has been highly unequal. With one exception (the Chaco War of 1932–35), there were no significant interstate wars (as distinct from civil wars) in the Western Hemisphere (the Americas) in the twentieth century. Enemy military operations have barely touched these territories: hence the shock of the bombing of the World Trade Center and the Pentagon on September 11, 2001. Since 1945, interstate wars have also disappeared from Europe, which had until then been the main battlefield region. Although in period III war returned to southeast Europe, it seems very unlikely to recur in the rest of the continent. On the other hand, during period II interstate wars, not necessarily unconnected with the global confrontation, remained endemic in the Middle East and South Asia, and major wars directly springing from the global confrontation took place in East and Southeast Asia (Korea, Indochina). At the same time, areas such as sub-Saharan Africa, which had been comparatively unaffected by war in period I (apart from Ethiopia, belatedly subject to colonial conquest by Italy in 1935–36), came to be theaters of armed conflict during period II, and witnessed major scenes of carnage and suffering in period III.

Two other characteristics of war in the twentieth century stand out, the first less obviously than the second. At the start of the twenty-first century we find ourselves in a world where armed operations are no longer essentially in the hands of governments or their authorized agents, and where the contending parties have no common characteristics, status, or objectives, except the willingness to use violence. Interstate wars dominated the image of war so much in periods I and II that civil wars or other armed conflicts within the territories of existing states or empires were somewhat obscured. Even the civil wars in the territories of the Russian Empire after the October Revolution, and those which took place after the collapse of the Chinese Empire, could be fitted into the framework of international conflicts, insofar as they were inseparable from them. On the other hand, Latin America may not have seen armies crossing state frontiers in the twentieth century, but it has been the scene of major civil conflicts: in Mexico after 1911, for instance, in Colombia since 1948, and in various Central American countries during period II. It is not generally recognized that the number of international wars has declined fairly continuously since the mid-1960s, when internal conflicts became more common than those fought between states. The number of conflicts within state frontiers continued to rise steeply until it leveled off in the 1990s.

More familiar is the erosion of the distinction

between combatants and noncombatants. The two world wars of the first half of the century involved the entire populations of belligerent countries; both combatants and noncombatants suffered. In the course of the century, however, the burden of war shifted increasingly from armed forces to civilians, who were not only its victims, but increasingly the object of military or military-political operations. The contrast between the First World War and the Second is dramatic: only 5 percent of those who died in World War I were civilians; in World War II the figure increased to 66 percent. It is generally supposed that 80 to 90 percent of those affected by war today are civilians. The proportion has increased since the end of the Cold War because most military operations since then have been conducted not by conscript armies, but by quite small bodies of regular or irregular troops, in many cases operating high-technology weapons and protected against the risk of incurring casualties. While it is true that high-tech weaponry has made it possible in some cases to reestablish a distinction between military and civilian targets, and therefore between combatants and noncombatants, there is no reason to doubt that the main victims of war will continue to be civilians.

What is more, the suffering of civilians is not proportionate to the scale or intensity of military operations. In strictly military terms, the two-week war between India and Pakistan over the independence of Bangladesh in 1971 was a modest affair, but it produced ten million refugees. The fighting between armed units in Africa during the 1990s can hardly have involved more than a few thousand, mostly ill-armed, combatants, yet it produced, at its peak, almost seven million refugees—a far greater number than at any time during the Cold War, when the continent had been the scene of proxy wars between the superpowers.

This phenomenon isn't confined to poor and remote areas. In some ways the effect of war on civilian life is magnified by globalization and the world's increasing reliance on a constant, unbroken flow of communications, technical services, deliveries, and supplies. Even a comparatively brief interruption of this flow—for instance, the few days' closure of U.S. airspace after September 11th—can have considerable, perhaps lasting, effects on the global economy.

It would be easier to write about the subject of war and peace in the twentieth century if the difference between the two remained as clear-cut as it was supposed to be at the beginning of the century, in the days when the Hague Conventions of 1899 and 1907 codified the rules of war. Conflicts were supposed to take place primarily between sovereign states or, if they occurred within the territory of one particular state, between parties sufficiently organized to be accorded belligerent status by other sovereign states. War was supposed to be sharply distinguished from peace, by a declaration of war at one end and a treaty of peace at the other. Military operations were supposed to distinguish clearly between combatants—marked as such by the uniforms they wore, or by other signs of belonging to an organized armed force—and noncombatant civilians. War was supposed to be between combatants. Noncombatants should, so far as possible, be protected in wartime. It was always understood that these conventions did not cover all civil and international armed conflicts, and notably not those arising out of the imperial expansion of Western states in regions not under the jurisdiction of internationally recognized sovereign states, even though some (but by no means all) of these conflicts were known as "wars." Nor did they cover large rebellions against established states, such as the so-called Indian Mutiny; nor the recurrent armed activity in regions beyond the effective control of the states or imperial authorities nominally ruling them, such as the raiding and blood feuding in the mountains of Afghanistan or Morocco. Nevertheless, the Hague Conventions still served as guidelines in the First World War. In the course of the twentieth century, this relative clarity was replaced by confusion.

First, the line between interstate conflicts and conflicts within states—that is, between international and civil wars—became hazy, because the twentieth century was characteristically a century not only of wars, but also of revolutions and the breakup of empires. Revolutions or liberation struggles within a state had implications for the international situation, particularly during the Cold War. Conversely, after the Russian Revolution, intervention by states in the internal affairs of other states of which they disapproved became common, at least where it seemed comparatively risk-free. This remains the case.

Second, the clear distinction between war and peace became obscure. Except here and there, the Second World War neither began with declarations of war nor ended with treaties of peace. It was followed by a period so hard to classify as either war or peace in the old sense that the neologism "Cold War" had to be invented to describe it. The sheer obscurity of the position since the Cold War is illustrated by the current state of affairs in the Middle East. Neither "peace" nor "war" exactly described the situation in Iraq since the formal end of the Gulf War—the country was still bombed almost daily by foreign powers— nor can the situation there since the 2003 invasion be made to fit the traditional meaning of war, though it is certainly not a peace in any sense. This also applies to the relations between Palestinians and Israelis, and those between Israel and its neighbors Lebanon and Syria. All this is an unfortunate legacy of the twentieth-century world wars, but also of war's increasingly powerful machinery of mass propaganda, and of a period of confrontation between incompatible and passion-laden ideologies which brought into wars a crusading element comparable to that seen in religious conflicts of the past. These conflicts, unlike the traditional wars of the international power system, were increasingly waged for nonnegotiable ends such as "unconditional surrender." Since both wars and victories were seen as total, any limitation on a belligerent's capacity to win that might be imposed by the accepted conventions of eighteenth-

and nineteenth-century warfare—even formal declarations of war—was rejected. So was any limitation on the victors' power to assert their will. Experience had shown that agreements reached in peace treaties could easily be broken.

In recent years the situation has been further complicated by the tendency in public rhetoric for the term "war" to be used to refer to the deployment of organized force against various national or international activities regarded as antisocial—"the war against the Mafia," for example, or "the war against drug cartels." Not only is the fight to control, or even to eliminate, such organizations or networks, including small-scale terrorist groups, quite different from the major operations of war, this use of the term also confuses the actions of two types of armed force. One—let's call them "soldiers"—is directed against other armed forces with the object of defeating them. The other—let's call them "police"—sets out to maintain or reestablish the required degree of law and public order within an existing political entity, typically a state. Victory, which has no necessary moral connotation, is the object of one force; the bringing to justice of offenders against the law, which does have a moral connotation, is the object of the other.

Such a distinction is easier to draw in theory than in practice, however. Homicide by a soldier in battle is not, in itself, a breach of the law. But what if a member of the Irish Republican Army (IRA) regards himself as a belligerent, even though official British law regards him as a murderer? Were the operations in Northern Ireland a war, as the IRA held, or an attempt in the face of lawbreakers to maintain orderly government in one province of the United Kingdom? Since not only a formidable local police force but a national army was mobilized against the IRA for thirty years or so, we may conclude that it was a war, but one systematically run like a police operation, in a way that minimized casualties and the disruption of life in the province. In the end, there was a negotiated settlement, one which, typically, for nine years brought not peace, but merely an extended absence of fighting. Such are the complexities and confusions of the relations between peace and war at the start of the new century. They are well illustrated by the military and other operations in which the United States and its allies are at present engaged.

There is now, as there was throughout the twentieth century, a complete absence of any effective global authority capable of controlling or settling armed disputes. Globalization has advanced in almost every respect—economically, technologically, culturally, even linguistically—except one: politically and militarily, territorial states remain the only effective authorities. There are officially about two hundred states, but in practice only a handful count, of which the United States is overwhelmingly the most powerful. However, no state or empire has ever been large, rich, or powerful enough to maintain hegemony over the political world, let alone to establish political and military supremacy over the globe. The world is too big, complicated, and plural. There is no likelihood that the United States, or any other conceivable single-state power, could establish lasting control, even if it wanted to.

A single superpower cannot compensate for the absence of global authorities, especially given the lack of conventions—relating to international disarmament, for instance, or weapons control—strong enough to be voluntarily accepted as binding by major states. Some such authorities exist, notably the United Nations, various technical and financial bodies such as the International Monetary Fund (IMF), the World Bank, and the World Trade Organization (WTO), and some international tribunals. But none has any effective power other than that granted to it by agreements between states, or thanks to the backing of powerful states, or voluntarily accepted by states. Regrettable as this may be, it isn't likely to change in the foreseeable future.

Since only states wield real power, the risk is that international institutions will be ineffective or lack universal legitimacy when they try to deal with offenses such as "war crimes." Even when world courts are established by general agreement (for example, the International Criminal Court set up by the U.N. Rome Statute of July 17, 1998), their judgments will not necessarily be accepted as legitimate and binding, so long as powerful states are in a position to disregard them. A consortium of powerful states may be strong enough to ensure that some offenders from weaker states are brought before these tribunals, perhaps curbing the cruelty of armed conflict in certain areas. This is an example, however, of the traditional exercise of power and influence within an international state system, not of the exercise of international law.

This is also the case, by definition, where individual states accept international humanitarian law and unilaterally assert the right to apply it to citizens of other countries in their national tribunals—as, notably, the Spanish courts, supported by the British House of Lords, did in the case of General Augusto Pinochet of Chile.

There is, however, a major difference between the twenty-first and the twentieth century: the idea that war takes place in a world divided into territorial areas under the authority of effective governments which possess a monopoly on the means of public power and coercion has ceased to apply. It was never applicable to countries experiencing revolution, or to the fragments of disintegrated empires, but until recently most new revolutionary or postcolonial regimes—China between 1911 and 1949 is the main exception—emerged fairly quickly as more or less organized and functioning successor regimes and states.

Over the past thirty years or so, however, the territorial state has, for various reasons, lost its traditional monopoly on armed force, much of its former stability and power, and, increasingly, the fundamental sense of legitimacy, or at least of accepted permanence, which allows governments to impose burdens such as taxes and conscription on willing citizens. The material equipment for warfare is now

27

widely available to private bodies, as are the means of financing nonstate warfare. In this way, the balance between state and nonstate organizations has changed.

Armed conflicts within states have become more serious and can continue for decades without any significant prospect of victory or settlement: Kashmir, Angola, Sri Lanka, Chechnya, Colombia. In extreme cases, as in parts of Africa, the state may have virtually ceased to exist; or may, as in Colombia, no longer exercise power over part of its territory. Even in strong and stable states it has been difficult to eliminate small unofficial armed groups, such as the IRA in Britain and ETA in Spain. The novelty of this situation is indicated by the fact that the most powerful state on the planet, having suffered a terrorist attack, feels obliged to launch a formal operation against a small, international, nongovernmental organization or network lacking both a territory and a recognizable army.

How do these changes affect the balance of war and peace in the coming century? I would rather not make predictions about the wars that are likely to take place or their possible outcomes. However, both the structure of armed conflict and the methods of settlement have been changed profoundly by the transformation of the world system of sovereign states.

The dissolution of the U.S.S.R. means that the Great Power system, which governed international relations for almost two centuries and, with obvious exceptions, exercised some control over conflicts between states, no longer exists. Its disappearance has removed a major restraint on interstate warfare and the armed intervention of states in the affairs of other states—foreign territorial borders were largely uncrossed by armed forces during the Cold War. The international system was potentially unstable even then, however, as a result of the multiplication of small, sometimes quite weak states, which were nevertheless officially "sovereign" members of the U.N. The disintegration of the U.S.S.R. and the European communist regimes plainly increased this instability. Separatist tendencies of varying strength in hitherto stable nation-states such as Britain, Spain, Belgium, and Italy might well increase it further. At the same time, the number of private actors on the world scene has multiplied. Under these circumstances, it is not surprising that cross-border wars and armed interventions have increased since the end of the Cold War.

What mechanisms are there for controlling and settling such conflicts? The record is not promising. None of the armed conflicts of the 1990s ended with a stable settlement. The survival of Cold War institutions, assumptions, and rhetoric has kept old suspicions alive, exacerbating the postcommunist disintegration of southeast Europe and making the settlement of the region once known as Yugoslavia more difficult.

These Cold War assumptions, both ideological and political, will have to be dispensed with if we are to develop some means of controlling armed conflict. It is also evident that the United States has failed, and will inevitably fail, to impose a new world order (of any kind) by unilateral force, however much power relations are skewed in its favor at present, and even if it is backed by an (inevitably short-lived) alliance. The international system will remain multilateral and its regulation will depend on the ability of several major units to agree with one another, even though one of these states enjoys military predominance. How far international military action taken by the United

States is dependent on the negotiated agreement of other states is already clear. It is also clear that the political settlement of wars, even those in which the United States is involved, will be by negotiation and not by unilateral imposition. The era of wars ending in unconditional surrender will not return in the foreseeable future.

The role of existing international bodies, notably the U.N., must also be rethought. Always present, and usually called upon, it has no defined role in the settlement of disputes. Its strategy and operation are always at the mercy of shifting power politics. The absence of an international intermediary genuinely considered neutral, and capable of taking action without prior authorization by the Security Council, has been the most obvious gap in the system of dispute management.

Since the end of the Cold War, the management of peace and war has been improvised. At best, as in the Balkans, armed conflicts have been stopped by outside armed intervention, and the status quo at the end of hostilities maintained by the armies of third parties. This sort of long-term intervention has been applied for many years by individual strong states in their sphere of influence (Syria in Lebanon, for instance). As a form of collective action, however, it has been used only by the United States and its allies (sometimes under U.N. auspices, sometimes not). The result has so far been unsatisfactory for all parties. It commits the interveners to maintain troops indefinitely, and at disproportionate cost, in areas in which they have no particular interest and from which they derive no benefit. It makes them dependent on the passivity of the occupied population, which cannot be guaranteed—if there is armed resistance, small forces of armed "peacekeepers" have to be replaced by much larger forces. Poor and weak countries may resent this kind of intervention as a reminder of the days of colonies and protectorates, especially when much of the local economy becomes dependent on the needs of the occupying forces. Whether a general model for the future control of armed conflict can emerge from such interventions remains unclear.

The balance of war and peace in the twenty-first century will depend not on devising more effective mechanisms for negotiation and settlement but on internal stability and the avoidance of military conflict. With a few exceptions, the rivalries and frictions between existing states that led to armed conflict in the past are less likely to do so today. There are, for instance, comparatively few burning disputes between governments about international borders. On the other hand, internal conflicts can easily become violent; the main danger of war lies in the involvement of outside states or military actors in these conflicts.

States with thriving, stable economies and a relatively equitable distribution of goods among their inhabitants are likely to be less shaky—socially and politically—than poor, highly inegalitarian, and economically unstable ones. A dramatic increase in economic and social inequality within, as well as between, countries will reduce the chances of peace. The avoidance or control of internal armed violence depends even more immediately, however, on the powers and effective performance of national governments and their legitimacy in the eyes of the majority of their inhabitants. No government today can take for granted the existence of an unarmed civilian population or the degree of public order long familiar in large parts of Europe. No government today is in a position to overlook or eliminate internal armed minorities. Yet the world is increasingly divided into states capable of administering their territories and citizens effectively—even when faced, as the United Kingdom was, by decades of armed action by an internal enemy—and a growing number of territories bounded by officially recognized international frontiers, with national governments ranging from the weak and corrupt to the nonexistent. These zones produce bloody internal struggles and international conflicts, such as those we have seen in Central Africa. There is, however, no immediate prospect for lasting improvement in such regions, and a further weakening of central government in unstable countries, or a further Balkanization of the world map, would undoubtedly increase the dangers of armed conflict.

A tentative forecast: war in the twenty-first century is not likely to be as murderous as it was in the twentieth. But armed violence, creating disproportionate suffering and loss, will remain omnipresent and endemic—occasionally epidemic—in a large part of the world. The prospect of a century of peace is remote.

III

War, Peace, and Hegemony
at the Beginning of
the Twenty-first Century

1

It is impossible to talk about the political future of
the world unless we bear in mind that we are living
through a period when history—that is to say, the
process of change in human life and society and the
human impact on the global environment—has been
accelerating at a dizzying pace. It is now proceeding
at a speed which puts the future of both the human
race and the natural environment at risk. In the
middle of the last century, we suddenly entered a
new phase in world history which has brought to
an end history as we have known it in the past ten
thousand years, that is to say since the invention of
sedentary agriculture. We do not know where we are
going.

I tried to sketch the outlines of this dramatic and sudden break in world history in my history of the "short twentieth century," published in 1994. The technological and productive transformations are obvious. Think only of the speed of the communications revolutions, which have virtually abolished time and distance. The Internet was barely ten years old in 2004. I also singled out four social aspects of it, which are relevant to the international future. These are the dramatic decline and fall of the peasantry, which had until the nineteenth century formed the great bulk of the human race as well as the foundation of its economy; the corresponding rise of a predominantly urban society, and especially what might be called the hyper-cities, with populations measured in eight digits; the replacement of a world of oral communication by a world of universal reading and writing by hand or machine; and, finally, the transformation in the situation of women.

The decline and fall of the agricultural part of humanity is obvious in the developed world. Today it amounts to 4 percent of the occupied population in members of the Organization for Economic Cooperation and Development (OECD)—2 percent in the United States. But it is evident elsewhere. In the mid-

1960s, there were still *five* states in Europe with more than half the occupied population in farming, *eleven* in the Americas, *eighteen* in Asia and, with three exceptions (Libya, Tunisia, and South Africa), all of Africa. The situation today is dramatically different. For practical purposes, no countries are left with at least half their populations on farms in Europe and the Americas, or indeed in the Islamic world—even Pakistan has fallen below 50 percent, while Turkey has fallen from a peasant population of three-quarters to one-third. Even the major fortress of peasant agriculture—Southeast Asia—has been breached in several places—Indonesia is down from 67 percent to 44 percent, the Philippines from 53 percent to 37 percent, Thailand from 82 percent to 46 percent, Malaysia from 51 percent to 18 percent. In fact, omitting most of sub-Saharan Africa, the only solid bastions of peasant society left—say, over 60 percent of the occupied population in 2000—are in the former South Asian empires of Britain and France—India, Bangladesh, Myanmar (Burma), and the Indochinese countries. But, given the acceleration of industrialization, how long will this last? In the late 1960s the farming population formed half of the population in Taiwan and South Korea: today it is down to 8 percent and 10 percent, respectively. Within a few decades we will have ceased to be what humanity has been since its emergence, a species whose members are chiefly engaged in gathering, hunting, or producing food.

We shall also cease to be an essentially rural species. In 1900, only 16 percent of the world's population lived in towns. In 1950 it had risen to just under 26 percent; today it is just under half (48 percent). In the developed countries, and in many other parts of the globe, the countryside, even in the agriculturally productive areas, is a green desert in which human beings are hardly ever visible outside motorcars and small settlements, until the traveler reaches the nearest town. But here extrapolation becomes more difficult. It is true that the old developed countries are heavily urbanized, but they are no longer typical of current urbanization, which takes the form of a desperate flight from the countryside into hyper-cities. What is happening to cities in the developed world—even the ones nominally growing—is the suburbanization of growing areas around the original center or centers. Today, only ten of the world's largest fifty cities are in Europe and North America, and only two of the eighteen world cities of ten million and more. The fastest-growing cities over one million are, with a single exception (Porto, in Portugal), in Asia (twenty), Africa (six), and Latin America (five). Whatever its other consequences, this dramatically changes the political balance, especially in countries with elected representative assemblies or presidents, between highly *concentrated* urban populations and geographically *spread-out* rural ones in states where up to half the population may live in the capital city, though nobody can say exactly how.

As to the educational transformation, the social and cultural effects of general literacy cannot easily be separated from the social and cultural effects of the sudden, and utterly unprecedented, revolution in the public and personal media of communication in which we are all engaged. Let me note only one significant fact. There are today twenty countries in which more than 55 percent of the relevant age groups continue studying after their secondary education. But with a single exception (South Korea) *all* of them are in Europe (old capitalist and ex-socialist), North America, and Australasia. In its capacity to generate human capital, the old developed world still retains a substantial advantage over the major new-comers of the twenty-first century. How fast can Asia, and particularly India and China, catch up?

I want to say nothing here about that greatest single social change of the past century, the emancipation of women, except for one observation supplementing what I have just said. The emancipation of women is best indicated by the degree to which they have caught up with or even surpassed the education of men. While this has made dramatic progress in most Western countries since the 1960s, it is still badly lagging in most parts of the developing world and, what is more troubling, actively impeded in some, though not all, parts of the Islamic region.

2

If one looks more closely at the factors affecting war, peace, and power at the outset of the twenty-first century, the general trends are not necessarily guides to practical realities. It is evident, for instance, that in the course of the twentieth century the world's population outside the Americas ceased to be over-whelmingly ruled, as it were, from the top down, by hereditary princes or the agents of a foreign power. It now came to live in a collection of technically independent states whose governments claimed legitimacy by reference to "the people" or "the nation," in most cases (including even the so-called totalitarian regimes), claiming confirmation by real or bogus elections or plebiscites and/or by periodic mass public ceremonies that symbolized the bond between authority and the people. One way or another people have changed from being *subjects* to *citizens;* including, in the twentieth century, not only men but women. But how close to reality does this get us, even today when most governments have, technically speaking, variants of liberal-democratic constitutions with contested elections, though sometimes suspended by military rule that is deemed to be temporary, but has often lasted a long time? Not very far.

Nevertheless, one general trend can probably be observed across most of the globe. It is the change in the position of the independent territorial state itself, which in the course of the twentieth century became the basic political and institutional unit under which human beings lived. In its original home in the North Atlantic region, it was based on *several* innovations made since the French Revolution. It had the monopoly of the means of power and coercion: arms, armed men, prisons. It exercised increasing control by a central authority and its agents of what takes place on the territory of the state, based on a growing capacity to gather information. The scope of its activity and its impact on the daily life of its citizens grew, and so did success in mobilizing its inhabitants on the grounds of their loyalty to state and nation. This phase of state development reached its peak forty years or so ago.

Think, on the one hand, of the "welfare state" of Western Europe in the 1970s, in which "public consumption"—that is, the share of the gross domestic product (GDP) used for public purposes and not private consumption or investment—amounted to between roughly 20 percent and 30 percent. Think, on the other hand, of the readiness of citizens not only to let public authorities tax them to raise such enormous sums, but actually to be conscripted to fight and die "for their country" in the millions during the great wars of the last century. For more than two centuries, until the 1970s, this rise of the modern state had been continuous, and proceeded irrespective of ideology and political organization—liberal, social democratic, communist, or fascist.

This is no longer so. The trend is reversing. We have a rapidly globalizing world economy based on transnational private firms, doing their best to live outside the range of state law and state taxes, which severely limits the ability of even big governments to control their national economies. Indeed, thanks to the prevailing theology of the free market, states are actually abandoning many of their most traditional direct activities—postal services, police, prisons, even important parts of their armed forces—to profit-making private contractors.[1] It has been estimated that 100,000 or more such armed "private contractors" are at present active in Iraq.[2] Thanks to this development and the flooding of the globe with small, but highly effective, weaponry during the Cold War, armed force is no longer monopolized by states and their agents. Even strong and stable states like Britain, Spain, and India have learned to live for long periods at a time with effectively indestructible, if not actually state-threatening, bodies of armed dissidents. We have seen, for various reasons, the rapid disintegration of numerous member states of the U.N., most but not all of them products of the disintegration of twentieth-century empires, in which the nominal governments are unable to administer or exercise actual control over much of their territory, population, or even their own institutions. Actual separatist movements are found even in old states like Spain and Britain.

Almost equally striking is the decline in the acceptance of state legitimacy, of the voluntary acceptance of obligation to ruling authorities and their laws by those who live on their territories, whether as citizens or as subjects. Without the readiness of vast populations, for most of the time, to accept as legitimate any effectively established state power—even that of a comparative handful of foreigners—the era of nineteenth- and twentieth-century imperialism would have been impossible. Foreign powers were at a loss only in the rare zones where this was absent, such as Afghanistan and Kurdistan. But, as Iraq demonstrates, the natural obedience of people in the face of power, even in the face of overwhelming military superiority, has gone, and with it the return of empires. But it is not only the obedience of subjects but of citizens that is rapidly eroding. I very much doubt whether *any* state today—not the United States, Russia, or China—could engage in major wars with conscript armies ready to fight and die "for their country" to the bitter end. Few Western states can any longer rely, as most so-called developed countries once could, on a population that was basically law-abiding and orderly, except for the expected criminal or other fringes on the margins of the social order. The extraordinary rise of technological and other means of keeping the citizens under surveillance at all times (by public cameras, phone-tapping, access to personal data and computers, and so on) has not made state power and law more effective in these states, though it has made the citizens less free.

All this has been taking place in an era of dramatically accelerated globalization—that is to say, of growing regional disparities within the globe. For globalization by its nature produces unbalanced and asymmetric growth. It also underlines the contradiction between those aspects of contemporary life which are subject to globalization and the pressures of global standardization—science and technology, the economy, various technical infrastructures, and, to a lesser extent, cultural institutions—and those which are not, notably the state and politics. For instance, globalization logically leads to a growing flow of labor migration from poorer to richer regions, but this produces political and social tension in a number of the states affected, mostly in the rich countries of the old North Atlantic region, even though in global terms this movement is modest:

even today only 3 percent of the world's people live outside the country of their birth. Unlike the movement of capital, commodities, and communications, states and politics have so far put effective obstacles in the way of labor migrations.

The most striking new imbalance created by economic globalization, apart from the dramatic deindustrialization of the old Soviet and East European socialist economies in the 1990s, is the growing shift of the center of gravity of the world economy from the region bordering the North Atlantic to parts of Asia. This is still in its early stages, but accelerating. There can be no doubt of the fact that the growth of the world economy in the past ten years has been pulled along largely by the Asian dynamos, notably the extraordinary rate of growth of industrial production in China—with a 30-percent rise in 2003 compared with 3 percent for the world, and less than .5 percent in North America and Germany.[3] Clearly this has not yet greatly changed the relative weight of Asia and the old North Atlantic—the United States, the European Union, and Japan between them continue to represent 70 percent of the global GDP— but the sheer size of Asia is already making itself felt. In terms of purchasing power, South, Southeast, and

East Asia already represent a market about two-thirds larger than the United States. How this global shift will affect the relative strength of the U.S. economy is naturally a question central to the international prospects of the twenty-first century. I shall return to it below.

3

Let me now move even closer to the problem of war, peace, and the possibility of an international order in the new century. At first sight it would seem that the prospects of world peace must be superior to those of the twentieth century, with its unparalleled record of world wars and other forms of death on an astronomic scale. And yet, a recent poll in Great Britain, which compares the answers of Britons in 2004 to questions asked in 1954, reveals that the fear of world war today is actually *greater* than it was then.[4] That fear is largely due to the increasingly evident fact that we live in an era of endemic worldwide armed conflict, typically fought within states, but magnified by foreign intervention. Though small in twentieth-century *military* terms, the impact of such conflicts on civilians—who have increasingly become their main victims—is relatively enormous, and long-lasting.

Since the fall of the Berlin Wall, we once again live in an era of genocide and compulsory mass population transfers, as in parts of Africa, southeastern Europe, and Asia. It is estimated that at the end of 2003 there were perhaps thirty-eight million refugees inside and outside their own country, which is a figure comparable to the vast numbers of "displaced persons" in the aftermath of World War II. One simple illustration: in 2000, the number of battle-related deaths in Myanmar (Burma) was no more than five hundred, but the number of the "internally displaced," largely by the activities of the Myanmar Army, was about one million.[5] The Iraq War confirms the point. Small wars, by twentieth-century standards, produce vast catastrophes.

The typical twentieth-century form of warfare, that between states, has been declining sharply. At the moment, no such traditional interstate war is taking place, although such conflicts cannot be excluded in various areas of Africa and Asia or where the internal stability or cohesion of existing states is at risk. On the other hand, the danger of a major global war, probably arising out of the unwillingness of the United States to accept the emergence of China as a rival superpower, has not receded, although it is not immediate. The chances of avoiding such a conflict sometime are better than the chances of avoiding World War II were after 1929. Nevertheless, such a war remains a real possibility within the next decades.

Even without traditional interstate wars, small or large, few realistic observers today expect our century to bring a world without the constant presence of arms and violence. However, let us resist the rhetoric of irrational fear with which governments like President Bush's and Prime Minister Blair's seek to justify a policy of global empire. Except as a metaphor, there can be no such thing as a war against terror or terrorism, but only against particular political actors who use what is a tactic, not a program. As a tactic terror is indiscriminate, and morally unacceptable, whether used by unofficial groups or states. The International Committee of the Red Cross recognized the rising tide of barbarism as it condemned both sides in the Iraq War. There is also much fear that biological killers may be used by small terrorist groups, but, alas, much less fear of the greater but unpredictable dangers if the new ability to manipulate the processes of life, including human life, escapes from control, as it surely will. However, the actual dangers to world stability, or to any *stable* state, from the activities of the Pan-Islamic terrorist networks against which America proclaimed its global war, or for that matter from the sum total of all the terrorist movements now in action anywhere, are negligible. Though they kill much larger numbers of people than their predecessors—if many fewer than states—the risk to life they present is statistically minimal. For the purpose of military aggression, they hardly count. Unless such groups were to gain access to nuclear weapons, which is not unthinkable, but not an immediate prospect, either, terrorism will call for cool heads, not hysteria.

4

And yet, the world disorder is real, and so is the prospect of another century of armed conflict and human calamity. Can this be brought under some kind of global control again, as it was for all but thirty years during the 175 years from Waterloo to the collapse of the U.S.S.R.? The problem is more difficult today for two reasons. First, the much more rapidly growing inequalities created by the uncontrolled free-market globalization are natural incubators of grievance and instability. It has recently been observed that "not even the most advanced military establishments could be expected to cope with a general breakdown of legal order"[6]—and the crisis of states to which I referred earlier makes such a general breakdown easier than it once was. And second, there is no longer a plural international Great Power system, such as actually was in a position to keep a general collapse into global war at bay, except for the age of catastrophe from 1914 to 1945. This system rested on the presumption, dating back to the treaties ending the Thirty Years' War of the seventeenth century, of a world of states whose relations were governed by rules, notably noninterference in one anothers' internal affairs, and on a sharp distinction between war and peace. Neither are any longer valid today. It also rested on the reality of a world of plural power, even in the small "first division" of states, the handful of Great Powers, reduced after 1945 to two superpowers. None could prevail absolutely, and (outside much of the Western Hemisphere) even regional hegemony always proved to be temporary. They had to live together. The end of the U.S.S.R. and the overwhelming military superiority of America have ended this power system. It has ceased to exist. What is more, U.S. policy since 2002 has denounced both its treaty obligations and the conventions on which the international system was based, on the strength of a probably lasting supremacy in high-tech offensive warfare, which has made it the only state capable of major military action in any part of the world at short notice.

The American ideologists and their supporters see this as the opening of a new era of world peace and economic growth under a beneficent global American Empire, which they compare, wrongly, to the *Pax Britannica* of the nineteenth-century British Empire. Wrongly, because historically empires have not created peace and stability in the world around them, as distinct from their own territories. If anything it was the absence of major international conflict that kept them in being, as it did the British Empire. As for the good intentions of conquerors and their beneficent results, they belong to the sphere of imperial rhetoric. Empires have always justified themselves, sometimes quite sincerely, in moral terms—whether they claimed to spread (their version of) civilization or religion to the benighted, or to spread (their version of) freedom to the victims of (someone else's) oppression, or, today, as champions of human rights. Patently, empires had some positive results. The claim that imperialism brought modern ideas into a backward world, which has no validity today, was not entirely spurious in the nineteenth century. However, the claim that it significantly accelerated the economic growth of the imperial dependencies will not bear much examination, at least outside the areas of European overseas settlement. Between 1820 and 1950, the mean per capita GDP of twelve Western European states multiplied by 4.5, whereas in India and Egypt it barely increased at all.[7] As for democracy, we all know that strong empires kept it at home; only declining ones conceded as little of it as they could.

But the real question is whether the historically unprecedented project of global domination by a single state is possible, and whether the admittedly overwhelming military superiority of the United States is adequate to establish it, and beyond this to maintain it. The answer to both questions is no. Arms have often established empires, but it takes more than arms to maintain them, as witness the old saw dating back to Napoleon: "You can do anything with bayonets except sit on them." Especially today, when even overwhelming military force no longer in itself produces tacit acquiescence. Actually, most historic empires have ruled indirectly, through native elites often operating native institutions. When they lose their capacity to win enough friends and collaborators among their subjects, arms are not enough. The French learned that even a million white settlers, an army of occupation of eight hundred thousand, and the military defeat of an insurgency by systematic massacre and torture were not enough to keep Algeria French.

So one might ask why America abandoned the policies which maintained a real hegemony over the greater part of the globe, namely the noncommunist and nonneutralist part, after 1945. Its capacity to exercise this hegemony did not rest on destroying its enemies or forcing its dependencies into line by the direct application of military power. The use of force was as then limited by the fear of nuclear suicide. American military power was relevant to the hegemony only insofar as it was seen as preferable to other military powers—that is to say, during the Cold War, the Europe of the North Atlantic Treaty Organization (NATO) wanted its support against the armed might of the U.S.S.R.

The American hegemony of the second half of the last century rested not on bombs but *economically* on the enormous wealth of the country and the central role its giant economy played in the world, especially in the decades after 1945. *Politically* it rested on a general consensus in the rich North that their societies were preferable to those under communist regimes, and, where there was no such consensus, as in Latin America, on alliances with national ruling elites and armies afraid of social revolution. *Culturally* it rested on the attractions of the affluent consumer society enjoyed and propagated by the country which had pioneered it and on Hollywood's world conquest. *Ideologically* America undoubtedly benefited as the champion and exemplar of "freedom" against "tyranny," except in those regions where it was only too obviously allied with the enemies of freedom.

All this could—and indeed did—easily survive the end of the Cold War. Why should others not look for leadership to the superpower which represented what most other states now adopted, electoral democracy—to the greatest of economic powers committed to the neoliberal ideology which was sweeping the globe? Its influence and that of its ideologists and business executives was immense. Its economy, though slowly losing its central role in the world and no longer dominant in industry, or even, since the

1980s, in direct foreign investments,[8] continued to be huge and to generate enormous wealth. Those who conducted its imperial policy had always been careful to cover the reality of U.S. supremacy over its allies in what was a genuine "coalition of the willing" with the emollient cream of tact. They knew that, even after the end of the U.S.S.R., the United States was not alone in the world. But they also knew they were playing the global game with cards they had dealt and by rules that favored them, and that no rival state of comparable strength and with global interests was likely to emerge. The first Gulf War, genuinely supported by the U.N. and the international community, and the immediate reaction to 9/11 demonstrated the post-Soviet strength of the U.S. position.

It is the megalomaniac American policy since 9/11 that has very largely destroyed the political and ideological foundations of the country's former hegemonic influence and left it with little to reinforce the heritage of the Cold War era but an admittedly frightening military power. There is no rationale for it. Probably for the first time in its history, an internationally almost isolated America is unpopular among most governments and peoples. Military strength underlines the economic vulnerability of a United

States whose enormous trade deficit is maintained by Asian investors, whose economic interest in supporting a falling dollar is rapidly diminishing. It also underlines the relative economic clout of others: the European Union, Japan, East Asia, and even the organized bloc of third-world primary producers. In the WTO the United States can no longer negotiate with clients. Indeed, may not the very rhetoric of aggression justified by implausible "threats to America" indicate a basic sense of insecurity about the global future of the United States?

Frankly, I can't make sense of what has happened in the United States since 9/11 that enabled a group of political crazies to realize long-held plans for an unaccompanied solo performance of world supremacy. I believe it indicates a growing crisis within American society, which finds expression in the most profound political and cultural division within that country since the Civil War, and a sharp geographical division between the globalized economy of the two seaboards, and the vast resentful hinterland, the culturally open big cities and the rest of the country. Today a radical right-wing regime seeks to mobilize "true Americans" against some evil outside force and against a world that does not recognize the uniqueness, the superiority, the manifest destiny of America. What we must realize is that American global policy is aimed inward, not outward, however great and ruinous its impact on the rest of the world. It is not *designed* to produce either empire or effective hegemony. Nor was the Donald Rumsfeld doctrine— quick wars against weak pushovers followed by quick withdrawals—designed for effective global conquest. Not that this makes it less dangerous. On the contrary. As is now evident, it spells instability, unpredictability, aggression, and unintended, almost certainly disastrous, consequences. In effect, the most obvious danger of war today arises from the global ambitions of an uncontrollable and apparently irrational government in Washington.

How shall we live in this dangerous, unbalanced, explosive world in the midst of major shifting of the social and political, national and international tectonic plates? As for governments, the best other states can do is to demonstrate the isolation, and therefore the limits, of actual U.S. world power by refusing, firmly but politely, to join further initiatives proposed by Washington which might lead to military action, particularly in the Middle East and Eastern Asia. To give America the best chance of learning to return from megalomania to rational foreign policy is the most immediate and urgent task of international politics. For whether we like it or not, America will remain a superpower, indeed an imperial power, even in what is evidently the era of its relative economic decline. Only, we hope, a less dangerous one.

IV

Why America's Hegemony Differs from Britain's Empire

1

History, we are told, is discourse. There is no understanding it unless we understand the language in which people think, talk, and make decisions about it. Among the historians tempted by what is called "the linguistic turn" there are even some who argue that it is the ideas and concepts expressed in the words characteristic of the period that explain what happened and why. The times we live in are saturated with what the philosopher Thomas Hobbes called "insignificant speech," speech which means nothing, and its subvarieties "euphemism" and George Orwell's "Newspeak," namely speech deliberately intended to mislead by misdescription. But unless the facts themselves change, no amount of changing names changes them.

The current debates about empire are good cases in point, even if we leave aside the element of spin or plain sanctimoniousness in the literature. These debates are about the implications of America's current claims to global supremacy. Those who favor the idea tend to argue that empires are good, those who do not tend to mobilize the long tradition of anti-imperialist arguments. But these claims and counter-claims are not really concerned with the actual history of empires. They are trying to fit old names to historical developments that don't necessarily fit old realities. This makes little historical sense. Current debates are particularly cloudy, because the nearest analogy to the world supremacy to which the United States government is committed is a set of words— "empire," "imperialism"—which are in flat contradiction to the traditional political self-definition of America, and which acquired almost universal unpopularity in the twentieth century. They are also in flat conflict with equally strongly held positive beliefs in the American political value system, such as "self-determination" and "law"—both domestic and international. Let us not forget that both the League of Nations and the United Nations were essentially projects launched and pressed through by American presidents. It is also troublesome that there is no historical precedent for the global supremacy that the American government has been trying to establish, and it is quite clear to any good historian and to all rational observers of the world scene that this project will almost certainly fail. The most intelligent of the neo-imperial school, that excellent historian Niall Ferguson, has no doubts about this probable failure, though, unlike me, he regrets it.

Four developments lie behind the current attempts to revive world empire as a model for the twenty-first century. The first is the extraordinary acceleration of globalization since the 1960s, and the tensions which have consequently arisen between the economic, technological, cultural, and other aspects of this process and the one branch of human activity which has so far proved quite impermeable to it, namely politics. Globalization in the currently dominant form of free-market capitalism has also brought a spectacular and potentially explosive rise in social and economic inequality within countries and internationally.

The second is the collapse of the international balance of power since World War II, which kept at bay both the danger of a global war and the collapse of large parts of the globe into disorder or anarchy. The end of the U.S.S.R. destroyed this balance, but I think it may have begun to fray from the late 1970s on. The basic rules of this system, established in the seventeenth century, were formally denounced by President Bush in 2002, namely that, in principle, sovereign states, acting officially, respected one anothers' borders and kept out of one anothers' internal affairs. Given the end of a stable superpower balance, how could the globe be politically stabilized? In more general terms, what would be the structure of an international system geared to a plurality of powers in which, at the end of the century, only one power was left?

The third is the crisis in the ability of the so-called sovereign nation-state—which in the second half of the twentieth century became the almost universal form of government for the world's population—to carry out its basic functions of maintaining control over what happened on its territory. The world has entered the era of inadequate, and in many cases failing or failed, states. This crisis also became acute from about 1970, when even strong and stable states like the United Kingdom, Spain, and France had to learn to live for decades with armed groups like the IRA, ETA, or Corsican separatists on their territories, lacking the power to eliminate them. In 2006, the Uppsala Conflict Data Bank of such things recorded incidents of armed civil war between 2001 and 2004 in thirty-one of the world's sovereign states.[1]

The fourth is the return of mass human catastrophe, up to and including the wholesale expulsion of peoples and genocide; and with it of general fear. We even have the reappearance of something like the medieval Black Death in the AIDS pandemic; the global nervousness about the potential extension of an "avian flu" that has, to date, killed no more than a few dozen humans; and the equivalent of eschatological hysteria in the tone of much public discussion on the effects of global warming. War and civil war have returned, even to Europe—there have been more wars since the fall of the Berlin Wall than during the whole of the Cold War period—but though the numbers who fight and their battle casualties are small compared to the mass wars of the twentieth century, their impact on the noncombatant population is disproportionately vast. At the end of 2004 it was estimated that there were almost forty million refugees outside and increasingly inside their own countries,[2] which is comparable to the number of "displaced persons" in the aftermath of World War II. Concentrated as they are in a few zones of the globe and now visible on-screen in our living rooms almost as they occur, these images of desolation have a far greater and immediate public impact in the rich countries than before. Think only of the reaction to the Balkan wars in the 1990s. Surely, people in the rich countries of the globe felt, something must be done about the appalling situation into which many of the poor parts of the globe seemed to be plunging.

In short, the world increasingly seemed to call for supranational solutions to supranational or transnational problems, but no global authorities were available with the ability to make policy decisions, let alone with the power to carry them out. Globalization stops short when it comes to politics, domestic or international. The United Nations has no independent authority or power, and depends on the collective decisions of *states*—not to mention that it can be blocked by the absolute veto of five of them. Even the international and financial organizations of the post-1945 world—the IMF, the World Bank—could take effective action only under Great Power patronage (the so-called Washington Consensus). The one body which could not, the General Agreement on Tariffs and Trade (GATT—since 1995 called the World Trade Organization, or WTO), has so far found state opposition an effective obstacle to agreement. The only effective actors are states. And, in terms of military power capable of major military action on a global scale, there is at present only one state capable of it, namely the United States.

2

"The best case for empire is always the case for order," it has been said.[3] In an increasingly disorderly and unstable world it is natural to dream of some power capable of establishing order and stability. Empire is the name of that dream. It is a historical myth. The American Empire, with its hopes of a *Pax Americana,* looks back to the assumed *Pax Britannica,* a period of globalization and world peace in the long nineteenth century associated with the assumed hegemony of the British Empire, and this in turn looked back to, and named itself after, the *Pax Romana* of the ancient Roman Empire. But this is claptrap. If the term "pax" has any meaning in this context it refers to the claim to establish peace *within* an empire and not internationally.

And even then it is largely phony. The empires of history rarely ceased to conduct military operations on their territory and certainly they did so on their frontiers at all times, only such operations rarely impinged on metropolitan civil life. In the era of nineteenth- and twentieth-century imperialism, usually wars against nonwhites or other "inferiors," Kipling's "lesser breeds without the law," were not counted as proper wars to which the usual rules applied. Hew Strachan rightly asks, "Where were the prisoners taken in British colonial conflicts, other than the Boer War [which was seen as a war between whites]? What judicial processes were regularly applied?"[4] President Bush's "unlawful combatants" in Afghanistan and Iraq, to whom neither law nor the Geneva Conventions apply, have their imperialist precedents.

As for world or even regional peace, it has been beyond the power of all empires known to history so far, and certainly beyond all Great Powers of modern times. If Latin America has been the only part of the world largely immune to major international wars for almost two hundred years, it is not due to the Monroe

Doctrine, which was "for decades ... little more than a Yankee bluff,"[5] or to U.S. military power, which was never in a position to directly coerce any state in South America. Until the time of writing it was habitually used only in the dwarf states of Central America and the islands of the Caribbean, and then not always directly. Military intervention, including attempts to impose "regime change," was practiced in Mexico (or what was left of it after the war of 1848) under President Wilson.[6] Disaster followed what has been described as his "program of moral imperialism," which "placed the weight of the United States behind a continuous, sometimes devious, effort to force the Mexican nation to meet his ill-conceived specifications" between 1913 and 1915.[7] However, since Wilson, Washington has decided, wisely, not to play armed Pentagon games with the only large country in its Caribbean backyard. It was not U.S. military power that brought about U.S. domination of the Western Hemisphere.

Britain, of course, as the phrase "splendid isolation" suggests, was always aware that it could not control the international power system of which it was a part, and had no significant military presence on the European continent. The British Empire benefited enormously from the century of peace between the powers, but it did not create it. I would summarize the relations between empires, war, and peace as follows: empires were mainly built, like the British Empire, by aggression and war. And in turn it was war—usually, as Niall Ferguson rightly points out, war between rival empires—that did them in. Winning big wars proved as fatal to empires as losing them: a lesson from the history of the British Empire which Washington might take to heart. International peace is not what they created, but what gave them a chance to survive. That superb book *Forgotten Armies* by Christopher Bayly and Tim Harper gives a vivid picture of how European power and hegemony in Southeast Asia, apparently so splendid and secure, collapsed in a matter of weeks in 1941 and 1942.[8]

3

All the same, leaving aside sixteenth-century Spain and perhaps seventeenth-century Holland, Britain from the mid-eighteenth to the mid-twentieth century and America since then are the only examples of genuinely global empires with global and not merely regional policy horizons and power resources—naval supremacy for nineteenth-century

Britain, supremacy in destruction by air for twenty-first-century America—each backed by a unique world network of suitable bases. This was and is not enough, since empires depend not just on military victories or security but on lasting control. On the other hand, nineteenth-century Britain and twentieth-century America also enjoyed an asset no previous empire had, or indeed could have had, in the absence of modern economic globalization. They dominated the industrial world economy. They did so not only by the size of their productive apparatus as "workshops of the world": America at its peak in the 1920s and again after World War II represented about 40 percent of the global industrial (manufacturing) output,[9] and currently still represents about a quarter of it (22–25 percent). Both empires also did so as economic models, technical and organizational pioneers, and trendsetters, and as the centers of the world system of financial and commodity flows and the states whose financial and trade policies largely determined the shape of these flows.

Both, of course, have also exercised disproportionate cultural influence, not least through the globalization of the English language. But cultural hegemony is not an indicator of imperial power, nor does it depend much on it. If it did, Italy, disunited, powerless, and poor, would not have dominated international musical life and art from the fifteenth through the eighteenth centuries. Moreover, where cultural power survives the decline of the power and prestige of the states that once propagated it, such as the Roman Empire or the French absolute monarchy, it is merely a relic of the past, like the French-derived military nomenclature or the metric system.

We must, of course, distinguish the direct cultural effects of imperial rule from those of economic hegemony, and both again from independent postimperial developments. The spread of baseball and cricket was indeed an imperial phenomenon, for these games are only played where once British soldiers or U.S. Marines were stationed. But this does not explain the triumph of the really global sports like soccer, tennis, or, for business executives, golf. They were all British nineteenth-century innovations, like practically all internationally practiced sports, including alpinism and skiing. Some (like Thoroughbred racing) may owe their organization and global spread to the international prestige of the nineteenth-century British ruling class, which also imposed its style of upper-class men's wear on the world,[10] just as the prestige of Paris imposed it on upper-class women's fashions. Others (notably soccer) had their original roots in the worldwide nineteenth-century diaspora of Britons hired to work for British firms abroad, yet others (golf) perhaps owe their success to the disproportionate share of Scots in imperial and economic development. Yet they have long outgrown their historic origins. It would be absurd to see the next soccer World Cup as an example of the "soft power" of Great Britain.

I now turn to the crucial differences between the two states. The potential size of the metropolitan country is the first obvious difference: islands like Britain have fixed borders. Britain had no frontier in the American sense. Britain has been part of a European continental empire on occasions—in Roman times, after the Norman conquest, and, for a moment, after Mary Tudor married Philip of Spain—but never the base of such an empire. When the countries of Britain generated surplus populations these populations migrated elsewhere or founded settlements overseas. The British Isles became a major source of emigrants. The United States was, and remains, essentially a receiver and not a sender of populations. It filled its empty spaces with its own growing population and with immigrants from abroad, until the 1880s mainly from northwestern and west-central Europe. With Russia (apart from the Pale of Jewish settlement) it is the only major empire which never developed a significant emigrant diaspora. Unlike Russia since its fragmentation in 1991, the United States still has not got one. Its expatriates form a smaller percentage of the population in OECD states than any other nation's expatriates, except those of Japan.[11]

The American Empire, it seems to me, is the logical by-product of this form of expansion across a continent. The young United States saw its republic as coterminous with all of North America. To settlers who brought to it the European expectations of farming population density, much of it seemed boundless and under used. Indeed, given the rapid, unintended quasi-genocide of the indigenous population by the impact of European diseases, much of it soon became so. Even so, one is surprised today that Frederick Jackson Turner's famous "frontier thesis" on the making of American history[12] found no place at all for the Native Americans, who, after all, had been very obviously present in the America of James Fenimore Cooper. North America was by no means "virgin land,"[13] but substituting the European form of economy for the indigenous and extensive use of the territory implied getting rid of the natives, even leaving aside the colonists' conviction that God had given the country exclusively to them. After all, the American Constitution specifically excluded the Native American from the body politic of "the people which enjoyed the birthright of" the "blessings of liberty."[14] Of course, effective elimination was possible only where the original population was relatively small, as in North America or Australia. Where it was not, as in Algeria, South Africa, Mexico, and, as it turned out, Palestine, even large settler populations had to live with, or rather on top of, large native populations.

Again, unlike Britain and all other European states, America never saw itself as one entity in an international system of rival political powers. That was precisely the system which the Monroe Doctrine claimed to exclude from the Western Hemisphere. Within that hemisphere of decolonized dependencies the United States had no rival. Nor did it have a concept of a colonial dependency, since all parts of the North American continent were to be integrated as parts of the United States sooner or later, even Canada, which it attempted but failed to detach from the British Empire. So it had problems with taking over adjacent territories that did not fit the pattern, mostly because they were not colonized or colonizable by white Anglos: Puerto Rico, Cuba, and the Pacific dependencies, for example. Among such territories only Hawaii was to make it to statehood. An independent slave South, being used to the difference between a free and a mass unfree population, and to integration into the British global trading system, might well have become more like a European empire, but it was the North that prevailed: free, protectionist, relying for its development on the unlimited mass home market. As it was, the characteristic form of U.S. empire outside its continental heartland was not to be like either the British Commonwealth or the British colonial empire. It could not consider dominions—that is, the gradual separation of areas of white settlement, with or without local natives (as in Canada, Australia, New Zealand, even South Africa)—because it sent no settlers abroad. In any case, since the North won the Civil War, the secession of any part of the Union was no longer legally and politically possible or on the ideological agenda. The characteristic form of U.S. power outside its own territory was not colonial, or indirect rule within a colonial framework of direct control, but a system of satellite or compliant states. This was all the more essential because U.S. imperial power until World War II was not global, but only regional—effectively confined to the Caribbean and the Pacific. So it was never able to acquire a wholly owned network of military power bases comparable to the British one, most of which is still there, though it has now lost all its old significance. To this day, several of the crucial bases of U.S. power abroad are technically on the soil of some other state which might—like Uzbekistan—withdraw permission for its use.

The second difference between the two states is that America is the child of a revolution—perhaps, as Hannah Arendt argued, of the most lasting revolution among the revolutions of the modern era, the ones driven by the secular hopes of the eighteenth-century Enlightenment.[15] If it were to acquire an imperial mission, it would be based on the messianic implication of the basic conviction that its free society was superior to all others, and destined to become the global model. Its politics, as Tocqueville saw, would inevitably be populist and antielitist. In Britain, both England and Scotland had their revolutions in the sixteenth and seventeenth centuries, but they did not last, and their effects were reabsorbed into a modernizing but socially hierarchical capitalist regime, governed until well into the twentieth century by kinship networks of a landowning ruling class. Colonial empire could easily be fitted into this framework, as it was in Ireland. Britain certainly had a strong conviction of its superiority to other societies, but absolutely no messianic belief in, or particular desire for, the conversion of other peoples to the British ways of government, or even to the closest thing to an ideological national tradition, namely anti-Catholic Protestantism. The British Empire was not built by or for missionaries; indeed, in its core dependency, India, it actively discouraged their activities.

Third, since the Domesday Book, the kingdom of England, and after 1707 Britain, was built around a strong center of law and government operating the oldest national state in Europe. Freedom, law, and social hierarchy went with a uniquely sovereign state authority, "the king in parliament." Note that in 1707 England entered a union with Scotland under a single central government, and not as a federal arrangement, even though Scotland remained separate from England in every other respect—law, state religion, administrative structure, education, even the sound of its language. In America, freedom is the adversary of central government, or indeed of any state authority, which is in any case deliberately crippled by the separation of powers. Compare the history of the American frontier with the very British history of its Canadian equivalent. The heroes of the U.S. Wild West are gunmen who make their own law of the John Wayne kind in lawless territory. The heroes of the Canadian West are the Mounties, an armed federal police force (founded in 1873) maintaining the state's law. After all, did not the British North America Act of 1867, which created the Dominion of Canada, state its object as "peace, order, and good government" and not "life, liberty, and the pursuit of happiness"?

Let me briefly mention one further difference between the two countries considered as nations: *age.* Along with a flag and an anthem, nation-states need a foundation myth for that modern construction, the nation, which is most conveniently provided by ancestral history. But America could not use ancestral history as a foundation myth, as England and even revolutionary France could—as even Stalin could use Alexander Nevsky to mobilize Russian patriotism against the Germans. America had no usable ancestors on its territory earlier than the first English settlers, since the Puritans defined themselves precisely as *not* being the Indians, and Native Americans, like slaves, were by definition outside the Founding Fathers' definition of "the people." Unlike the Spanish-American Creoles, they could not mobilize the memories of indigenous empires—Aztecs, Incas—in their struggle for independence. They could not integrate the heroic traditions of Native American warrior peoples, though their intellectuals admired them, if only because settler policy drove the most obvious candidates for cooption into an all-American ideology, the Iroquois Confederacy, mostly into alliance with the British. The only people linking its national identity to American Indians was European—the small and isolated Welsh, whose romantic explorers thought they had identified the descendants of Prince Madoc (who had, they felt sure, discovered America before Columbus) as notionally Welsh-speaking Mandans on the Missouri.[16] And since the United States was founded by revolution against Britain, the only continuity with the old country that was not shaken was cultural, or rather linguistic. But note that even here Noah Webster tried to break that continuity by insisting on a separate orthography.

So the national identity of America could not be constructed out of a common English past, even before the mass immigration of non-Anglo-Saxons. It had to be primarily constructed out of its revolutionary ideology and its new republican institutions. Most European nations have so-called hereditary others, permanent neighbors, sometimes with memories of centuries of conflict, against whom they define themselves. America, whose existence has never been threatened by any war other than the Civil War, has only ideologically defined enemies: those who reject the American way of life, wherever they are.

4

As with states, so with empires. Here also Britain and the United States are quite different. The empire—formal or informal—was an essential element both for Britain's economic development and its international power. It was not so for the United States. What was crucial for the United States was the initial decision to be not a state among other states, but a continental giant, eventually with a continental population. The land and not the sea was central to its development. America was expansionist from the start, but not in the ways of overseas maritime empires like the sixteenth-century Castilian and Portuguese, the seventeenth-century Dutch, and the British, which could be and usually were based on states of modest dimensions or populations. It was more like Russia, expanding outward across the plains from a central nucleus in Muscovy until it, too, could claim to reach "from sea to shining sea," namely from the Baltic to the Black Sea and the Pacific. America without an empire would still be the state with by far the largest population in the Western Hemisphere and the third-most-populated state on the globe. Even Russia, reduced as it now is to what it was before Peter the Great, remains a relative giant, not least in the natural resources available on its vast territory. Britain without its empire was and is just one middle-sized economy among many, and knew itself to be so even when it governed a quarter of the world's land and population.

What is more to the point, because the British

economy was essentially linked to global economic transactions, the British Empire was in many respects a central element in the development of the nineteenth-century world economy. This was not because it was a formal empire. There are no significant British colonial territories in Latin America outside the Caribbean area, and Britain deliberately refrained from using its naval or military force to intervene there, though it could easily have done so. And yet until World War I Latin America was far more a part of a British-oriented world economy than it was linked to the United States: British investments were more than twice as large as those of the United States in 1914,[17] and ran them close even in Mexico, where (with Cuba) American capital was concentrated.[18] In effect, nineteenth-century Britain was an economy complementary to the developing world. Through the 1950s, at least three-quarters of Britain's enormous investments were in developing countries[19] and even between the wars well over half of British exports went to the formal or informal British regions. That is why the British connection made the southern cone of Latin America prosperous while it lasted, while the U.S. connection with Mexico has produced chiefly a source of cheap labor for the northern neighbor. With European and U.S. industrialization, Britain soon ceased to be the world's workshop, except in the construction of the international transportation structure, but it remained the world's trader, the world's banker, the world's capital exporter. Nor should we forget that at the peak of its economic supremacy Britain had been in effect the world market for primary goods—food and raw materials. Modest as it was in size and population, as late as the 1880s it bought most of the internationally traded raw cotton and 35 percent of internationally traded wool. It consumed something like half of all internationally traded wheat and meat, and most of its tea.[20]

The American economy had and has no such organic connection with the world economy. Being by far the largest industrial economy on the globe, it made, and still makes, its impact through sheer continental size and the Yankee originality in technology and business organization that made it a model for the rest of the world from the 1870s on, especially in the twentieth century, when it emerged as the first society of mass consumption. Until the period between the wars, the U.S. economy, heavily protected, relied overwhelmingly on domestic resources and the domestic market. Unlike Britain, until the late twentieth century it was a relatively modest importer of commodities and a disproportionately small exporter of goods and capital. At the peak of its industrial power, in 1929, U.S. exports amounted to 5 percent of its GNP (in 1990 prices) as against 12.8 percent for Germany, 13.3 percent for the United Kingdom, 17.2 percent for the Netherlands, or 15.8 for Canada.[21] Indeed, in spite of its global industrial primacy from the 1880s on, with 29 percent of world industrial output, its actual share of global exports did not equal that of Britain until the eve of the 1929 stock-market crash.[22] It remains one of the least trade-dependent economies in the world—much less so than even the Euro area.[23] Although from World War I on the U.S. government encouraged American exporters by tax breaks and exemption from antitrust law,[24] U.S. enterprise did not seriously envisage penetrating into the European economies until the mid-1920s, and its advance was slowed by the Great Depression. Broadly speaking, the New World's economic conquest of the Old World is something that took place during the Cold War. There is no guarantee that it will last very long.

Unlike the world advances of nineteenth-century Britain, this conquest was only partly the result of what might be called the global division of labor between industrialized and developing (primary-goods-producing) countries. The great leap forward since World War II has been based on the increasingly globalized interchange between the similar and rival economies of developed industrial countries, which is why the gap between the developed and the poor worlds has widened so dramatically. But it is also why the plunge into free-market globalization makes even the strongest national economy dependent on forces it cannot control.

This is not the place to analyze the recent shift in the geographic distribution of economic power from its old centers on both sides of the Atlantic to the regions of the Indo-Pacific Oceans, nor their consequent vulnerability. Both these are evident enough. The historic advantages that allowed most of the inhabitants of North America, Japan, Australasia, and the favored parts of Europe, as the new century began, to enjoy a per capita GDP at least five times as high as the global mean[25] and a standard of living princely by the standards of 1900, and under unprecedented conditions of social security, are eroding. Those who in the past benefited disproportionately by a globalized market economy may cease to do so.

Those who pioneered globalization may become its victims. The greatest of the American advertising agencies that brought the twentieth-century way of marketing to the world, J. Walter Thompson, was taken over in 1987 by a British marketing service which now operates forty companies in eighty-three nations.

Faced with the industrialization of Europe and the United States, Victorian Britain (then still massively industrialized, still the world's largest trader and investor), shifted its markets and capital investments to the formal and informal empire. The United States of the early twenty-first century has no such option, and in any case could not exercise it, since it is no longer a major exporter of goods and capital, and pays for the vast demand for goods which it can no longer produce itself by going into debt to the new centers of world industry. It is the only major empire that has also been a major debtor. Indeed, with the exception of the seventy years between World War I and 1988,[26] the global bottom line of its economy has never been in credit. The capital assets, visible and invisible, accumulated since 1945 by the U.S. economy, are large and not liable to rapid erosion. Nevertheless, U.S. supremacy must be acutely vulnerable to its relative decline, and to the shift of industrial power, capital, and high technology into Asia. In a globalized world the "soft power" of market and cultural Americanization no longer reinforces American economic superiority. America pioneered supermarkets, but in Latin America and China the pace was set by the French Carrefour chain. The American Empire, unlike the British, has consistently had to rely on its political muscle.

American global enterprise was mixed with politics from the start, or at least from the moment that President Wilson addressed a convention of salesmen in Detroit in 1916, telling them that America's "democracy of business" had to take the lead in "the struggle for the peaceful conquest of the world."[27] No doubt its influence in the world rested both on being a model for business enterprise and its sheer size, and yet it also rested on its fortunate immunity to the catastrophes of two world wars, which exhausted the economies of Europe and the Far East, while the U.S. economy prospered. Nor were American governments unaware of the enormous boost this gave to dollar diplomacy. "We have got to finance the world in some important degree," said Woodrow Wilson, "and those who finance the world must understand it and rule it with their spirits and their minds."[28] During and after World War II, from the Lend-Lease of 1940 to the British loan of 1946, Washington policy did not conceal that it aimed at the weakening of the British Empire as well as victory over the Axis.

During the Cold War, the global growth of American enterprise took place under the patronage of the political project of the United States, with which most American CEOs, like most Americans, identified themselves. In return, given its world power, the government's conviction that U.S. law ought to prevail in the dealings of Americans anywhere in the world put considerable political force behind it. As the (often misquoted) 1950s phrase went, "What's good for the country is good for General Motors and vice versa." Of course, the first mass consumer economy benefited enormously from the rise of affluent European mass consumer societies in the golden decades of the 1950s and '60s. After all, it had developed the productive capacity, the big corporate producers, the institutions, the know-how, and even the language of such society. As a French novelist said as early as 1930, advertising sold not only the goods but the adjectives to talk about them. This, rather than the lucky fact that, thanks to the British Empire, English had the makings of a universal global language, is the essence of American cultural hegemony. Nevertheless, aside from its demonstration effect, the major contributions of America to twentieth-century world economic development were politically anchored: the Marshall Plan in Europe, the occupation land reforms in Japan, the military orders in Asia for the Korean and later the Vietnam War. Without the Cold War political supremacy in the "free world," would the sheer size of the American economy alone have been enough to establish the U.S. way of doing business, the U.S. credit-rating agencies, accountancy firms, and commercial contract practices, not to mention the "Washington Consensus" for international financing as the global standards? It may be doubted.

That is why the old British Empire is not and cannot be a model for the American project of world supremacy, except in one respect. Britain knew its limits, and especially the limits, present and future, of its military power. Being a middleweight country which knew that it could not hold the world heavyweight championship forever, it was saved from the megalomania that is the occupational disease of would-be world conquerors. It occupied and ruled a larger part of the globe and its population than any state has ever done or is likely to do, but it knew it did not and could not rule the world, and it did not try. Its navy, which did indeed enjoy supremacy on the oceans for a long time, was not a force suited to this purpose. Once Britain had established its global position by successful aggression and war, it kept out of the politics of European states as much as it could, and altogether out of those in the Western Hemisphere. It tried to keep the rest of the world stable enough to proceed with its own business, but did not tell it what to do. When the age of Western overseas empires ended in the mid-twentieth century, Britain recognized "the winds of change" earlier than other colonizers. And, because its economic position did not depend on imperial *power* but on trade, it adjusted more easily to its loss politically, as it had, after all, adjusted to the most dramatic setback in its earlier history, namely the loss of the American colonies.

Will the United States learn this lesson? Or will it be tempted to maintain an eroding global position by relying on politico-military force, and in so doing promote not global order but disorder, not global peace but conflict, not the advance of civilization but of barbarism? That, as Hamlet said, is the question. Only the future will show. Since historians are, fortunately, not prophets, I am not professionally obliged to give you an answer.

NOTES

Preface

1. *2007 KOF Index of Globalization*, Konjunkturforschung-
   sstelle ETH (Switzerland, 2007). (The rankings are based
   on the data for 2004.)

I: *On the End of Empires*

1. Jan Morris, "Islam's Lost Grandeur," review of *Salonica,
   City of Ghosts: Christians, Muslims and Jews, 1430–1950,* by
   Mark Mazower. *The Guardian* (London), September 18,
   2004, p. 9.

III: *War, Peace, and Hegemony at the Beginning of the Twenty-first Century*

1. Patrick Radden Keefe, "Iraq, America's Private Armies,"
   New York Review of Books, August 12, 2004, pp. 48–50.

---

2. See James Meek, "The Rise of the Private Army," *London Review of Books,* August 15, 2007, pp. 5–7.

3. Australia, France, Italy, the United Kingdom, and Benelux had negative growth. *CIA World Factbook* up to October 19, 2004.

4. *Daily Mail* (London), November 22, 2004, p .19.

5. Margareta Sollenberg, ed., *States in Armed Conflict, 2000* (Uppsala, 2001); *Internal Displacement: A Global Overview of Trends and Developments in 2003,* http://www.internal-displacement.org (accessed November 20, 2004).

6. John Steinbrunner and Nancy Gallagher, "An Alternative Vision of Global Security," *Daedalus* (Summer 2004): 84.

7. Angus Maddison, *L'économie mondiale 1820–1992. Analyse et Statistiques* (Paris: OECD, 1995), pp. 20–21. The figures for Egypt are only from 1900.

8. In 1980 it was on the order of 40 percent of the world's direct foreign investment, between 1994 and 2005 it averaged only 18 percent as against an average of 43 percent for the European Union. United Nations Conference on Trade and Development (UNCTAD), *World Economic Outlook* (Geneva, 2006), p. 19.

IV: *Why America's Hegemony Differs from Britain's Empire*

1. Centre for the Study of Civil War, Uppsala Conflict Data Project, *Armed Conflicts, 1945–2004,* http://prio.no/cwp/ArmedConflict (accessed June 17, 2006).

2. United Nations High Commissioner for Refugees (UNHCR), *The State of the World's Refugees: Human*

Displacement in the New Millennium (Oxford, 2006), cap. 7, figure 7.1.

3. Niall Ferguson, *Colossus: The Rise and Fall of the American Empire* (London, 2005), p. xxviii.

4. Hew Strachan, "Existential Struggle," review of *Absolute Destruction: Military Culture and the Practices of War in Imperial Germany*, by Isabel V. Hull; *Decisions for War, 1914–1917*, by Richard F. Hamilton and Roger H. Herwig; *Germany and the Causes of the First World War*, by Mark Hewitson; and *The Warlords: Hindenburg and Ludendorff*, by John Lee, in *Times Literary Supplement*, July 29, 2005.

5. Ferguson, *Colossus*, p. 42.

6. Friedrich Katz, *The Secret War in Mexico: Europe, the United States and the Mexican Revolution* (Chicago and London, 1981), cap. 5, pp. 156–202.

7. Howard F. Cline, *Mexico: Revolution to Evolution, 1940–1960* (Oxford, New York, Toronto, 1962), p. 141.

8. Christopher Bayly and Tim Harper, *Forgotten Armies: The Fall of British Asia, 1941–1945* (London, 2004).

9. League of Nations, *Industrialisation and Foreign Trade* (Geneva, 1943), p. 13.

10. Anne Hollander, *Sex and Suits: The Evolution of Modern Dress* (New York, 1994), pp. 102–103.

11. Jean-Christophe Dumont and Georges Lemaître, "Counting Immigrants and Expatriates in OECD Countries: A New Perspective," *OECD Social Employment and Migration Working Papers*, no. 25 (Paris: OECD, 2003/2006), chart 2, table 3.

12. Frederick Jackson Turner, "Western State-Making in the

Revolutionary Era," *American Historical Review* I (October 1, 1895): 70ff.

13. Henry Nash Smith, *Virgin Land: The American West as Symbol and Myth* (New York, 1957), pp. 154–57, 200.

14. Eric Foner, *The Story of American Freedom* (London, Basingstoke, and Oxford, 1998), p. 38.

15. Hannah Arendt, *On Revolution* (New York and London, 1963).

16. Gwyn A. Williams, *Madoc: The Making of a Myth* (Oxford, 1987).

17. Angus Maddison, *L'Economie Mondiale 1820–1992: Analyse et Statistiques* (Paris: OECD Development Centre, 1995), table 3.3.

18. Calculated from Herbert Feis, *Europe: The World's Banker, 1870–1914* (1931; repr., New York: Council on Foreign Relations, 1965), p. 23; and Cleona Lewis, *America's Stake in International Investments* (Washington, D.C., 1938), appendix D., p. 606. The dollar to pound exchange rate has been roughly estimated at 4.5 to 1.

19. Eric J. Hobsbawm with Christopher Wrigley, *Industry and Empire,* rev. ed. (London, 1999), table n32a.

20. Dr. F. X. von Neumann-Spallart, *Uebersichten der Weltwirthschaft, Jahrgang 1883–84* (Stuttgart, 1887), pp. 189, 226–27, 352–53, 364–66.

21. Angus Maddison, *The World Economy: A Millennial Perspective* (Paris: OECD Development Centre, 2001), appendix F, p. 5.

22. W. W. Rostow, *The World Economy: History and Prospect* (London and Basingstoke, 1978), pp. 72–73, 75.

23. *Economist, Pocket World in Figures,* 2004 ed. (London, 2003), p. 32.

24. Victoria de Grazia, *Irresistible Empire: America's Advance Through Twentieth-Century Europe* (Cambridge, Mass., and London, 2005), p. 213.

25. United Nations Development Program (UNDP), *World Report on Human Development* (Brussels, 1999), table 11.

26. Jeffry A. Frieden, *Global Capitalism: Its Fall and Rise in the Twentieth Century* (New York and London, 2006), pp. 132, 381.

27. de Grazia, *Irresistible Empire,* p. 1.

28. Frieden, *Global Capitalism,* p. 133.

About the Author

Eric Hobsbawm was Professor of Economic and Social History at Birkbeck College, University of London, from 1947 to 1982. He also taught at Stanford, M.I.T., Cornell, and the New School for Social Research from 1982 to 2001. A Fellow of the British Academy, the American Academy of Arts and Sciences, and the Japan Academy, he is the author of more than twenty books of history, including *The Age of Revolution, The Age of Capital, The Age of Empire,* and *The Age of Extremes.* In addition to eighteen honorary degrees from universities around the world, he has been the recipient of many prestigious prizes. He lives in London with his wife, Marlene.

A Note on the Type

This book was set in Tyfa, originally the winning design for a Czech typeface for book composition, made into fonts for Linotype and released in 1959. Designed by Josef Tyfa, it was popular in Czechoslovakia but little used elsewhere owing to communication difficulties during the Cold War, until another Czech designer started digitizing it under Tyfa's direction in 1995 for the International Typeface Corporation. Tyfa is based on classical form but is quirky and modern in nature.

Composed by Creative Graphics,
Allentown, Pennsylvania
Printed and bound by Thomson-Shore, Inc.,
Dexter, Michigan
Designed by Anthea Lingeman